My State UTAH

By Christina Earley

TABLE OF CONTENTS

A Crabtree Seedlings Book

Crabtree Publishing

crabtreebooks.com

School-to-Home Support for Caregivers and Teachers

This book helps children grow by letting them practice reading. Here are a few guiding questions to help the reader build his or her comprehension skills. Possible answers appear in red.

Before Reading:

- What do I know about Utah?
  - *I know that Utah is a state.*
  - *I know that Utah has many lakes.*
- What do I want to learn about Utah?
  - *I want to learn which famous people were born in Utah.*
  - *I want to learn what the state flag looks like.*

During Reading:

- What have I learned so far?
  - *I have learned that Salt Lake City is the state capital of Utah.*
  - *I have learned that Zion National Park has more than 78 kinds of mammals.*
- I wonder why...
  - *I wonder why the state flower is the sego lily.*
  - *I wonder why Bear Lake is a turquoise-blue color.*

After Reading:

- What did I learn about Utah?
  - *I have learned that you can kayak on Lake Powell.*
  - *I have learned that the state animal is the Rocky Mountain elk.*
- Read the book again and look for the glossary words.
  - *I see the word **capital** on page 6, and the word **seal** on page 12. The other glossary words are found on pages 22 and 23.*

UTAH
Hi! My name is Gideon. Welcome to Utah!

I live in Garden City. I can see tall mountains from my house.

My city is next to Bear Lake. The lake is known for its beautiful turquoise-blue color.

Utah is in the western United States. The **capital** is Salt Lake City.

Fun Fact: Salt Lake City is the largest city in Utah.

The state animal is the Rocky Mountain elk.

The sego lily is the state flower.

We grow a lot of cherries in Utah. Some of them are used to make cherry pie.

Fun Fact: Utah grows around 2 billion cherries a year.

My state flag is blue. The state **seal** is in the middle.

My family enjoys watching the Utah Jazz play basketball.

I like to visit Zion National Park. Zion Canyon is beautiful.

Fun Fact: There are more than 78 kinds of **mammals** at the park.

I can kayak on Lake Powell.

I have fun hiking at **Arches** National Park. The park has more than 2,000 stone arches.

Dancer Julianne Hough was born in Utah. Former NFL quarterback Steve Young was also born in Utah.

Fun Fact: Philo Farnsworth, the **inventor** of the first electronic TV system, was born in Beaver, Utah.

My favorite place to ski is Park City Mountain Resort.

I enjoy swimming at Homestead Crater. It is a **hot spring** inside a cave!

Glossary

arch (ahrch): Something with a curved shape and an opening underneath

capital (cap-ih-tuhl): The city or town where the government of a country, state, or province is located

hot spring (hot spring): A place where hot water flows out of the ground

inventor (in-vent-er): A person who creates something that did not exist before

mammal (mam-uhl): A warm-blooded animal that has hair or fur, and that feeds milk to its young

seal (seel): A special design that is used on important papers and other items

Index

About the Author

Christina Earley lives in sunny South Florida with her husband and son. She enjoys traveling around the United States and learning about different historical places. Her hobbies include hiking, yoga, and baking.

Written by: Christina Earley
Designed and Illustrated by: Bobbie Houser
Series Development: James Earley
Proofreader: Melissa Boyce
Educational Consultant: Marie Lemke M.Ed.

Photographs:
Alamy: JPA/AFF-USA: p. 18 right; Archive PL: p. 19, 23; Media Drum World: p. 21-22
Newscom: Ringo Chiu/ZUMAPRESS: p. 13
Shutterstock: prochasson frederic: cover; evenfh: p. 3; Jacob Boomsma: p. 4; MH Anderson Photography: p. 5; Volina: p. 6, 22; Sean Pavone: p. 7; Peter Wey: p. 8; salilbhatt: p. 9; overcrew: p. 10-11; Alena Levykin: p. 11; Millenius: p. 12, 23; Fotos593: p. 14-15; RMF: p. 15, 23; Maiza dos Santos: p. 16; TRphotos: p. 17, 22; Kathy Hutchins: p. 18 left; David A Litman: p. 20

Crabtree Publishing

crabtreebooks.com 800-387-7650

Printed in the U.S.A./072023/CG20230214

Published in Canada
Crabtree Publishing
616 Welland Avenue
St. Catharines, Ontario
L2M 5V6

Published in the United States
Crabtree Publishing
347 Fifth Avenue
Suite 1402-145
New York, New York, 10016

Library and Archives Canada Cataloguing in Publication
Available at Library and Archives Canada

Library of Congress Cataloging-in-Publication Data
Available at the Library of Congress

Hardcover: 978-1-0398-0537-8
Paperback: 978-1-0398-0569-9
Ebook (pdf): 978-1-0398-0633-7
Epub: 978-1-0398-0601-6